ADVICE
TO MY SON

ADVICE
TO MY SON

IBN AL-JAWZI

Translated by
Mokrane Guezzou

CLARITAS
BOOKS

1 2 3 4 5 6 7 8 9 10

CLARITAS BOOKS

Bernard Street, Swansea, United Kingdom
Milpitas, California, United States

CLARITAS
BOOKS

First Published in Jnauary 2019

Typeset in Minion Pro 14/11

Advice to My Son
By Ibn al-Jawzi
Translated by Mokrane Guezzou

A CIP catalogue record for this book is available from the British Library

ISBN: 978-1-905837-05-2

CONTENTS

FOREWORD

Allah Most High says in the Noble Quran: *Believers, guard yourselves and your families against a Fire whose fuel is men and stones, and over which are harsh, terrible angels who disobey not Allah in what He commands them and do what they are commanded* [al-Tahrim 66: 6]. It is also reported that the Leader of the Believers, Ali ibn Abi Talib, may Allah be well pleased with him, said: 'Teach yourselves and your families goodness.'[1] This is because teaching goodness to oneself and one's family is one of the foundations upon which the first Muslim community was built. As such, Muslims today will never prosper except by adhering to that which made their pious predecessors prosper.

The Prophet, may Allah bless him and grant him peace, is the role model of all Muslims when it comes to teaching goodness to members of one's household. He is reported to have said to his beloved daughter Fatima, may Allah be well pleased with her: 'O Fatima bint Muhammad! Save yourself from the Fire, for I will avail you nothing with Allah.'[2] He, may Allah bless him and grant him peace, also advised his cousin 'Abd Allah ibn Abbas, may Allah be well pleased with father and son, with a wonderful, blessed counsel which combines all goodness. He said, may Allah bless him and grant him peace: 'O lad! I will teach you a few things: watch out for Allah and Allah will watch out for you. Watch out for Allah and you will find Him before you. When you make a request, make it to Allah, and when you seek help, seek it from Allah. And know that if the whole nation were to gather to benefit you with something, they would not benefit you except with something that Allah has decreed for you. And if the whole nation were to gather to harm you with something, they would not harm you except with something that Allah has decreed for you. The pens have been lifted and the scrolls have dried.'[3] Ibn Abbas did indeed benefit from this priceless counsel and became the scholar par excellence of the whole Muslim Umma and the interpreter of the Quran (Turjuman al-Quran).

The wonderful counsel that we present here for the first time in translation is by a famous and prolific Muslim scholar who was considered the 'Preacher of the Whole World' and the 'Pride of Iraq'. His sessions of preaching softened numerous hard hearts, converted hundreds of non-Muslims to Islam and caused thousands of Muslim sinners and transgressors to repent. In his sessions of preaching, the heedless came back to their senses and remembered Allah, the ignorant masses learnt their religion and the disobedient gave up their evil ways. But this pious and godly scholar was not deluded with himself. He used to entreat his Lord with these words: 'O Allah! Have mercy on a person whose tears are shed out of regret for what he missed out from You; and on a soul which is burning because of its remoteness from You. O my Lord! O my Lord! My knowledge of Your good favour makes me hold out hope in You; and my certainty in Your overwhelming power makes me find solace in You Whenever I lift the veil of longing for You, diffidence vis-à-vis You holds it back. O my Lord! To You do I abase myself! By You I lower myself, and to You do I lead others!' So great was his insignificance before his Master and his fear of his Lord's chastisement that he wrote in *Sayd al-Khatir*: 'I sat down one day and saw around me about ten thousand people. There was not a single one of them except that his heart had softened up or his eyes shed tears. I said to myself: "What if they are all saved and you are damned?" So I cried with the tongue of my entire being: "O my Lord and Master! If You decree that I be chastised tomorrow, do not let them know of my chastisement, not for my sake, but out of regard for Your generosity, lest they say: He has chastised someone who guided others to Him."'[4]

Abul-Faraj Ibn al-Jawzi al-Hanbali, the author of this counsel, was born in 509 or 510 AH and died on 12 Ramadan 597 AH. His father died when he was three years old, so his paternal aunt took charge of his upbringing. When he grew to an age which allowed him to seek knowledge, his aunt took him to a scholar by the name of Ibn Nasir who taught him a great deal. He grew fond of preaching and, in fact, started preaching to people when still a teenager.

He was known from an early age for his religiosity. He did not mix with other children and did not consume anything doubtful. He ventured out from home only to go to the mosque. His resolve was such that he sought knowledge, preached and authored books all his life.

Ibn al-Jawzi studied under a multitude of scholars whom he mentions in his book *Mashyakhat Ibn al-Jawzi*. In this book, he mentions a great number of scholars from whom he benefitted in Hadith through his association with his teacher Ibn Nasir, and in Quran and its auxiliary sciences as well as the belle-letters through his association with the grandson of al-Khayyat and Ibn al-Jawaliqi. The last teachers from whom he reported Hadith are al-Dinawari and al-Mutawakkili.

A number of eminent figures studied under him, including his son Muhyi al-Din Yusuf, his son Ali al-Nasikh, his grandson Yusuf ibn Farghali al-Hanafi, the author of *Mir'at al-Zaman*, the Hafiz Abd al-Ghani, Shaykh Muwaffaq al-Din Ibn Qudama, Ibn al-Dubaythi and many others.

His grandson Abul-Muzaffar and most of those who wrote biographical entries of him mention that Ibn al-Jawzi had three surviving sons. The first one was Abu Bakr Abd al-Aziz, his eldest, who studied fiqh according to the Hanbali School of law, and Hadith from Abul-Waqt, Ibn Nasir, al-Armawi and some of his father's teachers. He later travelled to Mosul where he met some renown and was esteemed by people due to his preaching. He died in 554 AH in the lifetime of his father. The second one was Abul-Qasim Badr al-Din Ali al-Nasikh, for whom Ibn al-Jawzi wrote the present advice. The third one was Muhammad Yusuf Muhyi al-Din who succeeded his father in preaching. He grew up to be a fine scholar of sacred knowledge and wrote some books[5] before being given the office of Head of Market Inspection (hisba) in Baghdad. He was then appointed as an emissary of kings, especially to the Ayyubid sultans in the Levant. Later in life, in 640 AH, he was appointed as a professor at the Mu'tasimiyya University and he remained there until he was crucified, along was his three sons (Jamal al-Din, Sharaf al-Din and Taj al-Din), by the Mongols upon their invasion of Baghdad in 656 AH. This particular son was dutiful to his father throughout his life, unlike his brother Abul-Qasim for whom the present epistle was written.

As for the son for whom this counsel is addressed, Abul-Qasim Badr al-Din Ali al-Nasikh, he was born in the year 551 AH, thirty years before the birth of his brother Yusuf Muhyi al-Din. He studied Hadith with Abul-Fath al-Batti, Yahya ibn Thabit, Abu Zura,

Ahmad ibn al-Muqarrab, the vizier Ibn Hubayra and Shuhda. He reported Hadith from a number of Hadith transmitters, including al-Sayf, Izz al-Din Abd al-Rahman al-Maqdisi, al-Taqi al-Wasiti, al-Kamal Ali ibn Waddah, Abul-Faraj ibn al-Zayn, Abul-Abbas al-Faruthi and Shams al-Din Muhammad ibn Hubayra.

This particular son seems to have been studious in his early years and of good character. In fact, he preached to the masses for a period of time while still a boy. This indicates that his beginnings and upbringing was similar to that of his father. However, in the period before the birth of his brother Yusuf Muhyi al-Din in the year 580 AH, he seems to have faced a difficult phase in his life, which made him leave preaching, become idle and even engage in what is not permissible. Unfortunately, he did not immediately heed his father's counsel and continued for a while in his bad ways, through keeping the company of the corrupt and his inclination to amusement and debauchery. As a consequence, his father cut him off and disavowed him. But there is evidence he changed and eventually repented from his bad ways. The grandson of Ibn al-Jawzi, as well as a number of historians, mention that it was this particular son who prayed on his father upon the death of the latter, something which would have been impossible had he not changed his ways. Abul-Qasim Badr al-Din died in the year 630 AH.---

AUTHOR'S INTRODUCTION

On the Reason for Writing this Counsel

All praise be to Allah who originated the first father from dust, brought out his offspring from [between] breast-bones and loins, strengthened different clans through kinship and lineages, gracefully bestowed upon me knowledge and knowing what is right and proper, raised me well in my childhood and protected me in my youth, and gave me children through whose existence I hope to get abundant reward: *My Lord, make me a performer of the prayer, and of my seed. Our Lord, and receive my petition. Our Lord forgive You me and my parents, and the believers, upon the day when the reckoning shall come to pass* [Ibrahim 14: 40-41].

To proceed: Indeed, when I realised the nobility of

marriage and seeking offspring,[6] I completed a full recitation of the Quran[7] and asked Allah to give me ten children. Allah granted my request and I had five boys and five girls. Two of the girls and four of the boys died; and of the boys, only my son Abul-Qasim remained. I therefore asked Allah Most High to bring through him righteous descendants and realise through him all hopes and successes. However, I later saw in him a kind of slackness in seeking sacred knowledge. So I wrote for him this epistle to prompt and move him to tread my path in acquiring sacred knowledge, and guide him to take refuge in Him who grants success, may He be exalted and glorified, despite my knowledge that none can bring failure on the one whom Allah gives success and none can guide the one He sends astray. Nevertheless, Allah Most High says: *and counsel each other unto the truth, and counsel each other to be steadfast* [al-ʿAsr 104: 4] and: *therefore remind, if the reminder profits* [al-Aʿla 87: 9]. There is no mobility or strength except through Allah, the Most High, the Exalted.

A WORD TO AWAKEN DESIRE
AND INSTIL FEAR

You should know, O my dearest son, may Allah guide you to what is correct and proper, that human beings are specifically distinct from other created beings through their reasoning faculty only in order for them to act according to it. So summon your reasoning faculty, apply your mind and have a quiet moment with yourself and you shall know, with proofs, that you are a morally-responsible created being, that there are obligations you are required to fulfil, that the two angels enumerate and write down all you say and see, that the breathes of any living person are his steps towards his end-term and that one's stay in this world is short, one's confinement in the grave is very long and that the chastisement for acting according to one's whims and desires is severe. Where is yesterday's pleasure? Gone! What remains is only regret. Where is the desire of the ego? How many people have suffered a relapse because of it? And how many feet have slipped due to succumbing to it?

No-one acquires felicity except through opposing his desires and no-one becomes damned except by preferring this world. So take admonishment from bygone kings and ascetics: where is the pleasure of the former and the toil of the latter? What remain of both are abundant reward and good mention for the righteous and nothing but despicable mention and severe punishment for the sinners. It is as if the hungry of the past were never hungry, and those who filled their bellies were never full. Being slack in performing virtues is an evil companion, while love of leisure bequeaths the kind of regret that exceeds any pleasure. So beware and toil for yourself!

You should also know that performing what is obligatory and shunning what is prohibited is imperative. When a person transgresses, he will have nothing but hellfire to face.

Then you should know that seeking virtues is the ultimate objective sought by those who strive hard. Nonetheless, virtues vary. Some people estimate that virtues lie in non-attachment to this world, while others think they lie in preoccupying oneself with worship. In reality, though, perfect virtues lie in the combination of knowledge and action. When knowledge and action happen, they raise the person who has them to realising knowledge of the Creator Most High and move him to love Him, fear Him and long for Him. This is the intended goal, and strictness in matters varies amongst different people, while not every seeker is sought and not everyone who is looking for something will find it. However, the servant has to strive and 'everyone is facilitated in what he is created for,'[8] and help is only sought from Allah.

OBLIGATIONS, VIRTUES
AND HIGH RESOLVE

The first thing that should be looked into is to know Allah Most High with proof. It is well known that if a person sees the sky high above and the earth down below and observes the structures which are perfectly executed, especially in his own body, such a person will necessarily know that any craft must have a craftsman and any building must have a builder.

Then one must reflect on the proof of the truthfulness of the Messenger, may Allah bless him and grant him peace. The greatest of these proofs is the Quran which disbelievers have failed to come up with the like of a single *Sura* of it. When the existence of the Creator Most High and the truthfulness of the Messenger, may Allah bless him and grant him peace, are established, one must submit one's entire being to the Sacred Law. If one does not do so, this implies that there is a flaw in one's belief.

Then one must know what is incumbent upon them of the ritual ablution, the prayer, the poor-due – if one has wealth – the pilgrimage as well as other obligations. So when one knows the extent of the obligation, one does it.

The person of resolve ought to rise to engaging in virtuous acts and deeds, occupying himself with the memorisation of the Quran and its exegesis, and with the Hadith of the Messenger, Allah bless him and grant him peace, and with knowing his life and the lives of his Companions and of the Ulema after them, so that he opts for the higher rank and then the highest. He must also know that by which his tongue is set right in terms of grammar and some useful parts of language.

Islamic law (*fiqh*) is the basis of all Islamic disciplines, while preaching is the sweetest and most profitable. I have written books on all the disciplines mentioned above such that you will not need the books of old scholars on these disciplines or any other books, by the grace and bounty of Allah.[9] Thus, I have spared you the need to look for books or to focus your resolve on writing them yourself. One's resolve halts only because of its despicable character, otherwise when one's resolve is high, one is not content with what is less.

I have come to realise, with proof, that the human being is born with an innate resolve. Some resolves sometimes fall short, but they march forward when prompted. So when you see some failure in yourself, ask the Bestower of graces; and if you see slackness in yourself, seek help from the One who grants success. This is because you will never attain any good except through obeying Him and you will never miss any good except through disobeying Him. Is there any person who betook himself to Allah and did not get everything he sought? And is there any person who turned away from Allah and got any benefit or acquired any of his objectives? Have you not read the verses of the poet:[10]

By Allah, I have never come to visit you
Except that I traverse great distances in no time.
And never have I turned away from your door
Except that I have abysmally failed.

AND FEAR ALLAH, AND
ALLAH TEACHES YOU[11]

O my dearest son, look at yourself vis-à-vis the limits set by Allah, so that you observe how you guard them. This is because he who takes care of them is taken care of, while he who neglects them is left abandoned. In what follows I shall mention some of my circumstances, in the hope that you may look at my striving and ask the One who granted me success; for most of the graces bestowed upon me were not acquired by me, but rather came through the providence of the All Gentle One and His solicitude towards me.

I remember myself possessing a high resolve at the age of six[12] while still at Quranic school associating with boys and older men. I was given an ample mind which was greater than the minds of old men. I do not remember having ever played in the streets with other children or laughing excessively.[13]

This was my practice to the extent that, at about the age of seven, I used to go to the court of the main mosque, but I never sat at the study circle of any charlatan. Instead, I used to seek the Hadith master who related the biographies of the narrators of Hadith. I memorised everything he said and then I went home and wrote down everything I heard. It was also around this time that our master Abul-Fadl Ibn Nasir,[14] may Allah have mercy on him, took me under his wing. He used to take me to other scholars of sacred knowledge and I heard from him the *Musnad* [of Imam Ahmad] and other major collections of Hadith. But at this stage of my life I did not know what was expected of me. He helped me by letting me read to him all the narrations I heard and, when I reached the age of puberty, he gave me the highest authorisation of transmission of Hadith.[15] I kept his company until he died, may Allah have mercy on him, and in the process I learnt from him the discipline of Hadith and transmission of traditions.

Boys were in the habit of going down to the River Tigris to enjoy the view from over the bridge. But in my early years, I used to go there with a book, and sit out of the view of people, on the side of al-Raqqa, occupying myself with knowledge.[16]

Then I was inspired to tread the way of non-attachment to this world and fasted continuously, reducing in the process my intake of food. I also forced myself to be steadfast. I therefore persevered, rolled up my sleeves and stayed awake at night. I did not confine myself to any one discipline. Rather, I studied Islamic law, the art of preaching to people and Hadith. I followed the ascetics and then I studied grammar. There was no session of any scholar teaching Hadith or preaching to people except that I attended, nor any out-of-town, visiting teacher save that I learnt from him. I always opted for virtuous acts and deeds. And when two matters were presented to me, I always followed the rightest of the two.

Allah Most High directed my steps in life as well as my personal growth in the best possible manner. He made me follow what was more appropriate for me and drove away from me enemies, resentful enviers and plotters. He made easy for me the means of acquiring sacred knowledge and sent me books whence I did not expect. He granted me understanding, swift memorisation, good handwriting and excellent composition of books. He never made me need anything of this world. Rather, he provided for me sustenance that is just enough to live on or even more. He also made my acceptance in the hearts of people easy, in fact more than is usual, such that my words affected them a great deal and their genuineness was never doubted. More than two hundred dhimmis[17] accepted Islam at my hand and more than one hundred thousand people repented from their bad ways in my assemblies.

I used to go running to different scholars to hear Hadith to the point I was out of breath upon arrival to their sessions, because I did not want others to be there before me. Oftentimes, I woke up in the morning with no food to eat and, when the night came, I had no food to eat either. However, Allah never abased me to any other created being. Rather, He drove my sustenance towards me to preserve my honour. Indeed, it would take me too long to explain my different states in this context. You can see for yourself now how my circumstances have turned out. And I can summarise it all for you in one sentence: *And Fear Allah, and Allah Teaches You* [al-Baqara 2: 282].

PRESERVING ONE'S TIME AND
SEIZING ONE'S MOMENTS

O my dearest son! Wake up and have regret vis-à-vis what you have neglected in the past! Strive to catch up with the perfected among men as long as you still have time. Water your bough as long as it is still moist. And remember the moments you wasted as it is a sufficient admonition: the pleasure of lassitude has gone and with it are gone degrees of virtuous deeds. The righteous predecessors, may Allah have mercy on them, used to like combining all virtuous deeds and they bitterly cried for missing even a single one of them. Ibrahim ibn Adham,[18] may Allah have mercy on him, said: 'We visited a worshipper in his sickness and found him looking at his feet and weeping. We asked him: "Why are you crying?" he said: "They are not covered in dust for the sake of Allah.'" Another worshipper was seen crying, so he was asked: 'Why are you crying?' He said: 'I cry for a day that has gone without me fasting it and for a night that has elapsed without me standing to pray throughout it.'

You should know, O my dearest son, that the days unravel hours and the hours unleash breaths and every breath is a chest-draw. So beware of exhaling a single breath without engaging in something useful, lest you see an empty chest-draw on the Day of Judgement and regret it. It is related in this context that a man said to Amir ibn Abd Qays:[19] 'Wait so that I can talk to you.' He responded by saying: 'Hold the sun still [and I will stop to talk to you]!' It is also related that a group of people sat with Maruf al-Karkhi,[20] may Allah have mercy on him, for quite some time so he said to them: 'Do you not want to leave? The angel in charge of the sun is unrelentingly dragging it.' It is reported in a Prophetic saying that: 'Whoever says: "Glory be to Allah the

Mighty and praise is due to Him", a palm tree is planted for him in Paradise.'[21] So think about the person who wastes his hours: how many palm trees is he going to miss?

The righteous predecessors used to seize their moments. Kahmas,[22] may Allah have mercy on him, used to complete the recitation of the Quran three times during any one day and night. There were also forty men among the righteous predecessors who prayed the morning prayer (*Subh*) with the ritual ablution they performed for the last prayer of the previous night *(Isha)*.[23] Rabia al-Adawiyya[24] used to stay awake all night engaged in worship and, when the dawn broke, she dozed off for just a few moments, only to quickly wake up in panic, saying: 'sleep in the grave is very long.'

THE PRICE OF
EVERLASTING LIFE

Any person who reflects on this world will realise that, before he or she was born, a long period of time had elapsed. If this person ponders on this world after he or she dies, this person will also realise that it will go on for a long time. This person will also know that the stay in the graves is very long. And when this person ponders on the Day of Judgement, he or she will know that it is fifty thousand years. If this person reflects on the abodes of Paradise and Hell, he or she will realise that they are endless. But if he or she goes back and thinks about his or her stay in this world, let us say sixty years[25] for example, this person will realise that thirty years of the total is spent on sleeping, and fifteen years of these sixty are years of childhood. When one counts the remaining years, one realises that most of them are devoted to desires, food and earning a living. If one extracts from all these years what one has set aside for the afterlife, one will find in it a great deal of showing off and heedlessness. So with what can one buy everlasting life? Indeed, the only price is these moments that constitute one's life.

VIGILANCE AFTER
HEEDLESSNESS

O my son! Do not despair of goodness because of your past neglect, for there are many people who have woken up after long slumber. Shaykh Abu Hakim,[26] may Allah have mercy on him, related to me the following. He said: 'In my early years I was busy with idleness and did not pay attention to sacred knowledge. One day, my father Abu Abd Allah al-Hadrami, may Allah have mercy on him, summoned me. He said to me: "O my dearest son, I am not going to live on and support you forever. So take these twenty gold coins and open for yourself a bakery to live on." So I said: "What talk is this?" He said: "Then, open a cloth shop!" I said: "You say this to me when I am the son of one of the judges working under the

Chief Judge Abd Allah al-Damaghani."[27] He said: "But I do not see you seeking sacred knowledge!" So I said: "Start teaching me right now." And he did. From then on I devoted myself to seeking sacred knowledge and Allah Most High made it easy for me.'

One of the companions of Abu Muhammad al-Halawani,[28] may Allah have mercy on him, related to me that he said the following: 'My father died when I was twenty-one years old. I used to be known for idleness and wasting my time on nothing. It happened that I went to court to complain about the residents of a house that I had inherited and overheard them say: "Here comes the good-for-nothing!" I said to myself: "So this is what they say about me!" I went back to my mother and said to her: "If you want me, you can find me in the mosque of Abu al-Khattab."[29] I kept the company of this shaykh and did not leave except to assume the office of judge, which I practised for a period of time.' I myself saw him delivering religious edicts and debating intricate religious issues.

A PEDAGOGICAL METHOD FOR
THE DAY AND NIGHT

O my dearest son! Take it upon yourself to wake up at dawn and avoid thereupon any talk about this world. This is because the righteous predecessors, may Allah have mercy on them, used to avoid talking about matters of this world at that particular time.

Say upon waking up from sleep: 'Praise be to Allah who brought me back to life after having slain me and to Him is the resurrection'[30] and: 'Praise be to Allah Who holds back heaven lest it should fall upon the earth, save by His leave. Surely Allah is All-Gentle to men, All-Compassionate.'[31]

Then get up to perform the ritual ablution and pray the *sunna* of *Fajr*.[32] You can then proceed to the mosque in all humility, saying on your way: 'O Allah! I ask You by the right of the supplicants upon You and by the right of this walk of mine – indeed, I did not leave the house in a mood of impertinence, arrogance, conceitedness or showing off but in order to ward off Your wrath and seek Your good pleasure – I ask You to shield me from Hell and to forgive my sins, for none forgives sins except You.'[33]

Proceed to pray on the right hand side of the imam.[34] Upon completing your pray, say: 'There is no god save Allah, alone without any associate, His is the dominion, to Him belongs all praise, He gives life and causes death, all goodness is in His Hand, and He has power over everything,' ten times.[35] Then say 'Glory be to Allah' ten times, 'Praise be to Allah' ten times and 'Allah is the greatest' ten times,[36] followed by the Verse of the Throne.[37] Then ask Allah Most High to accept your prayer. If it is adequate, remain seated and remember Allah Most High until the sun rises a little in the horizon. Then pray what is prescribed for you, and it is good if you pray eight units of prayer.[38]

SACRED KNOWLEDGE IS BETTER THAN
ANY SUPEREROGATORY ACT

Once you complete the revision of your lessons around the time of late midmorning, you should pray the prayer of midmorning (*Salat al-Duha*) which is eight units of prayer. Then occupy yourself with reading or writing down your lessons until the time of *Asr*. After which you should go back to your lessons, from after the prayer of *Asr* until the time of *Maghrib*. After *Maghrib*, you should perform two units of prayer in which you recite two parts of the Qur'an (*juz'ayn*). Once you perform the prayer of *Isha*, you should go back to your lessons,[39] and then you should lie down on your right hand side[40] and say: 'Glory be to Allah' thirty-three times, 'Praise be to Allah' thirty-three times and 'Allah is the greatest' thirty-four times.[41] After this you say: 'O Allah protect me from Your chastisement on the day You gather Your servants.'[42]

Once you open your eyes after sleep, you should know that your body has had its share of rest. You should therefore get up to perform ritual ablution and pray in the dark of night as much as you can, starting with two light units of prayer and then two more units in which you recite two parts of the Quran. Then you should go back to studying sacred knowledge because knowledge is better than any supererogatory act.[43]

CAUTION AGAINST DEFECTS
AND HINDRANCES

Adhere to seclusion for it is the origin of all good[44] and beware of evil companions. Let your companions be books and reflection on the lives of the righteous predecessors. Likewise, do not occupy yourself with learning a new discipline until you have mastered the discipline you are already engaged in learning. Behold the lives of the perfected ones in knowledge and action and never be content with what is less. One poet said:

I have never seen in people's defects anything
Like the shortcoming of those capable of perfection.

And you should know that sacred knowledge raises

the lowly among people. A great many scholars had no lineage to mention or outward form to admire. 'Ata ibn Abi Rabah,[45] for example, was very dark and of repulsive physical constitution but when Sulayman ibn Abd al-Malik,[46] the Caliph of all Muslims, and his two sons went to ask him about the rituals of the pilgrimage, he spoke with them while his head was turned away from them. So the caliph said to his two sons: 'Let us go! And you should never be lax or lazy in seeking sacred knowledge, for I will never forget our abasement in front of this black slave.'

Al-Hasan al-Basri,[47] Ibn Sirin,[48] Makhul[49] as well as numerous other eminent scholars were all clients [i.e. emancipated slaves or descendents of emancipated slaves] but gained status and honour through their sacred knowledge and God-consciousness.

ABSTENTION FROM WHAT
PEOPLE POSSESS

O my dearest son! Try your utmost to protect your honour against exposing yourself to seeking this world and abasing yourself to those who possess it. Be content and you will be honoured and esteemed.[50] It was once said: 'Whoever is content with bread and herbs cannot be enslaved by anyone.' It is related that a Bedouin Arab visited Basra and asked: 'Who is the master of this town?' They said: 'al-Hasan al-Basri.' He asked again: 'In what manner has he become their master?' They said: 'He freed himself from the need for their world but they are in need of his knowledge.'[51]

You should also know, O my dearest son, that my father was quite comfortable financially and left behind thousands of dinars worth of properties. When I reached the age of puberty, I was given twenty gold coins and two houses. This was all my inheritance. So I spent the gold coins on books of sacred knowledge and sold the two houses and spent the proceeds on the cost of seeking sacred knowledge. I had nothing left of the wealth I inherited. But your father was never humiliated in the course of seeking sacred knowledge, nor has he gone out from one township to another or sent any request to anyone asking him for financial help. All his matters followed the right course: *And whosoever fears God, He will appoint for him a way out, and He will provide for him from whence he never reckoned* [al-Talaq 65: 2-3].

IF GOD-CONSCIOUSNESS IS GENUINE
ONE EXPERIENCES EVERY GOOD

O my dearest son! If your God-consciousness is genuine, you shall see every good. However, the God-conscious person does not show off, nor expose himself to that which harms his religion. Whoever preserves the limits set by Allah, Allah will preserve him. The Messenger of Allah, may Allah bless him and grant him peace, said to Ibn Abbas, may Allah be well pleased with father and son: 'Watch out for Allah and Allah will watch out for you. Watch out for Allah and you will find Him before you...'[52]

You should know, O my dearest son, that because the provisions of the Prophet Yunus, peace be upon him, were good, he was saved from hardship through them. Allah Most High says: *Now had he not been of those that glorify God, he would have tarried in its belly until the day they shall be raised* [al-Saffat 33: 143-144]. As for the Pharaoh, because his provisions were no good, he could not find a way out when he faced hardship: *Now? And before you did rebel* [Yunus 10: 91]. So make for yourself good provisions of God-consciousness and you shall experience its effect. It is narrated in the Prophetic saying: 'No young man has God-consciousness in his youth except that Allah raises his rank in his old age.'[53] Allah Most High says: *And when he was fully grown, We gave him judgment and knowledge. Even so We recompense the good-doers* [Yusuf 12: 22], *Whosoever fears God, and is patient – surely God leaves not to waste the wage of the good-doers* [Yusuf 12: 90].

You should know that the best of these provisions are lowering one's gaze from what is unlawful, holding back one's tongue from excessive talk, observing the limits set by Allah and preferring Allah Most High over the whims of the ego. You already know the tradition of the three men who entered a cave and were trapped inside by a boulder that fell and blocked the entrance. One of them said: 'O Allah! I had my parents and children. I used to wait on my parents, holding the milk for them, until they drank, before giving the milk to my children. If I did that for Your sake, then set us free.' And so the boulder moved a little [but not enough for the men to get out]. The second man said: 'O Allah! I had hired a hireling who turned out to be displeased with his payment. So I invested his money in trade. And one day he came and said to me: "Will you not fear Allah and give me my money?" I said: "Go to those cows and shepherds and take them." If I did that for Your sake, then set us free.' And so the boulder moved a little [but not enough for the men to get out]. The third man said: 'O Allah! I was very attached to a cousin of mine. I once drew near her, but she said: "Fear Allah! And do not deflower me except through the right way of marriage." I held back [on hearing her words]. If I did that for Your sake, then set us free.' And so the boulder moved a little, enough for the men to get out.[54]

It is reported that Sufyan al-Thawri,[55] may Allah be well pleased with him, was seen in a dream. He was asked: 'How did you fare with Allah?' He said: 'I found myself the moment I was put in the grave before the Lord of the worlds. I entered in and heard someone say: "Sufyan?" I said: "Sufyan!" the voice said: "Do you remember the day when you preferred Allah over your desire?" I said: "Yes!" So the serving trays of Paradise took me.'

ON THE CONDUCT OF THE RIGHTEOUS PREDECESSORS

Your resolve ought to rise to the height of perfection, for some people have stopped at asceticism and some occupied themselves with sacred knowledge, but only rare figures combined perfect knowledge with perfect practice.

And know that I have studied the conducts of the Followers of the Prophet's Companions, as well as those who came after them, and I have not found anyone who achieved ample perfection than four men: Sa'id ibn al-Musayyib,[56] al-Hasan al-Basri, Sufyan al-Thawri and Ahmad ibn Hanbal,[57] may Allah be well pleased with them all. They were real men. These four had resolves that we fall short off. However, there were among the righteous predecessors a great number of people who had high resolves. So if you want to look into their states, you can refer to our book, *Sifat al-Safwa*.[58] If you wish, check the reports about Sa'id, al-Hasan, Sufyan and Ahmad, may Allah be well pleased with them, for I have compiled a separate book for each one of them.

MEMORISATION IS
YOUR CAPITAL

You already know, O my dearest son, that I have authored one hundred books.[59] Among these books is *al-Tafsir al-Kabir*[60] in twenty volumes, *al-Tarikh* in twenty volumes, *Tahdhib al-Musnad* in twenty volumes, while the remaining books vary between four and five volumes or a little more or less. With these, I have spared you the need to borrow other books or make any effort to author your own. So make sure to memorise what you have learnt, for memorisation is your capital and its use for different purposes is your profit. In both cases, however, be true in seeking refuge with Allah Most High by observing the limits He has set. Allah Most High says: *if you help Allah, He will help you* [Muhammad 47: 6], *So remember Me, and I will re-member you* [al-Baqara 2: 152], *and fulfil My covenant and I shall fulfil your covenant* [al-Baqara 2: 40].

Beware of stopping at the outer form of sacred knowledge without putting it into practice. Those who frequent the assemblies of princes and those who en-dear themselves to worldly people have turned away from practising what they know and, thus, are deprived of its blessing and benefit.

KNOWLEDGE AND PRACTICE
ARE INSEPARABLE

Beware of occupying yourself with devotion to worship without sacred knowledge, for a great number of ascetics and would-be Sufis have erred from the path of guidance when they acted without knowledge.[61]

Cover yourself with two garments of clothes such that you do not stand out amongst worldly people due to their expensiveness or amongst the ascetics because of their cheapness. Take yourself to account upon every look, word or step you make, for you are responsible for that. Moreover, the listeners will benefit in commensuration with your benefit from the knowledge you have learnt. If the preacher does not act upon his own knowledge, his preaching will bounce off the hearts of people as water bounces off hard stones.

Therefore, do not admonish others except with a good intention, do not walk about except with a good intention and do not eat a morsel of food except with a good intention. This matter will be revealed to you by reading about the good manners of the pious predecessors.

SOME SPLENDID
RECOMMENDED BOOKS

Make sure to read the book, *Minhaj al-Muridin*,[62] for it will teach you spiritual wayfaring. Let it be your sitting companion and teacher. Read also through *Sayd al-Khatir*[63] for you will come across events in it that will correct the matters of both your world and religion. And memorise the book *Junnat al-Nazar*, for it will be sufficient in sharpening your understanding of matters relating to Islamic law. And if you acquaint yourself with the book entitled *al-Hada'iq*,[64] it will inform you about most of the Prophetic traditions, while if you turn to the book entitled *al-Kashf*,[65] it will reveal to you what is hidden in the two rigorously authenticated collections of al-Bukhari and Muslim.

Do not busy yourself with the commentaries of the Quran authored by non-Arabs. My books *al-Mughni* and *Zad al-Masir* have not left out anything you might need in Quranic exegesis. As for what I have compiled of books on preaching, you will not need any other books on the subject at all.[66]

CHARACTERISTICS OF THE BENEFICIAL PREACHER

You should also be sociable with people while at the same time staying away from them. For seclusion is a rest from evil companions and a means of safeguarding one's dignity. The preacher, specifically, ought not to be seen displaying vulgar manners, walking in the marketplace or laughing excessively, so that people have a good opinion of him and benefit from his preaching.[67] If you are forced to mix with people, then do so while overlooking their shortcomings, for if you were to test their manners, you would not be able to be sociable with them.

DISCHARGING RIGHTS

Discharge the right of anyone who has a right on you, whether it is spouse, offspring or kin. Consider every moment you have and on what it is expended. Make sure that you expend it on nothing save the most honourable possible thing. And do not neglect yourself; let yourself become habituated with the most noble and best works. Send to your grave that which will please you when you eventually get there. As one poet said:

> *O you who's busy with this world of his*
> *And is deluded with long hope!*
> *Death only suddenly comes,*
> *And the grave is the box of works.*

Consider the consequences of any matter, so that your patience in the face of everything you crave for or dislike becomes insignificant in your eyes. If you feel heedlessness, go to the graveyards and remind yourself of your imminent departure from this world. And plan – and Allah is the real Planner – your expenditures without being spendthrift, so that you do not need others. This is because preserving wealth is a religious obligation, 'That you leave something for your heirs is better than them needing other people.'[68]

A GOOD CONCLUSION

You should know, O my dearest son, that we are descendants of Abu Bakr al-Siddiq, may Allah be well pleased with him,[69] and our father is al-Qasim ibn Muhammad ibn Abd Abi Bakr, may Allah be well pleased with him.[70] His history is documented in the book *Sifat al-Safwa*. Our ancestors then occupied themselves with trade and buying and selling. Of the ones who came of late, none was given the resolve to seek sacred knowledge except me, and now you. Try hard not to disappoint my opinion of you or what I hope for you. I hand you over to Allah Most High, and it is Him Whom I ask to give you success in both knowledge and action.

This is the most I can offer in this counsel of mine,

and there is no might except through Allah the Exalted, the Mighty. Praise be to Allah who gives more to those who praise Him, and may Allah's blessings and peace be upon our master Muhammad and upon his household and Companions.

SELECTED REFERENCES

- Aluji Abd al-Hamid al-, *Muallafat Ibn al-Jawzi*, Baghdad, 1975.
- Asfahani, Abu Nu'aym al-: *Hilyat al-Awliya' wa-Tabaqat al-Asfiya'*. Beirut: Dar al-Kutub al-'Il-miyya, 2007.
- A'zami, Muhammad Mustafa: *Studies in Hadith Methodology and Literature*. Kuala Lumpur: Islamic Book Trust, 2002.
- Dhahabi, Shams al-Din al-: *Siyar A'lam al-Nubalaa'*. Beirut: Mu'assasat al-Risala, 1985.
- Ibn Abd al-Barr Abu 'Amr Yusuf Ibn Abd Allah: *Jami' Bayan al-'Ilm wa-Fadlih*. Damam: Dar Ibn al-Jawzi, 1994.

- Ibn Abi Shayba Abu Bakr: *Musannaf.* Riyadh: Maktabat al-Rushd, 1409 AH.
- Ibn Abi Ya'la, Abu al-Husayn Muhammad al-Fara' al-Hanbali: *Tabaqat al-Hanabila.* Riyadh: Maktabat al Malik Fahd, 1419.
- Ibn al-'Imad Shihab al-Din: *Shadharat al-Dhahab.* Damascus and Beirut: Dar Ibn Kathir, 1986.
- Ibn al-Jawzi, Abul-Faraj: *Sayd al-Khatir.* Riyadh: Dar Ibn Khuzayma, 1997.

  : *Zad al-Masir fi 'Ilm al-Tafsir.* Damascus and Beirut: al-Maktab al-Islami and Dar Ibn Hazm, 2002.

  : *al-Mudhish.* Beirut: Dar al-Kutub al-'Ilmiyya, 2005.

  : *al-Kashf li-Mushkil al-Sahihayn.* Riyadh: Dar al-Watan, 1997.

  : *Manaqib al-Imam Ahmad.* Riyadh: Dar Hijr, 1409 AH.

  : *Sifat al-Safwa.* Cairo: Dar al-Hadith, 2009.

  : *al-Qussas wa'l-Mudhakkirin.* Beirut: al-Maktab al-Islami, 1983.

: *Tadhkirat al-Huffaz.* Beirut: Dar al-Kutub al-'Ilmiyya, n.d.

- Ibn al-Mulaqqin, Siraj al-Din Abu Hafs 'Umar: *aTabaqat al-Awliya.* Cairo: Maktbat al-Khanji, 1994.
- Ibn Kathir, Imad al-Din Abul-Fida: *al-Bidaya wa'l-Nihaya.* Beirut: Maktabat al-Ma'arif, 1983.
- Ibn Khallikan, Abul-Abbas Shams al-Din Ahmad: *Wafayat al-A'yan wa-Anba' Abna' al-Zaman.* Beirut: Dar Sadir, different dates.
- Ibn Rajab Zayn al-Din Abu'l-Faraj al-Hanbali: *Lata'if al-Ma'arif fima li-Mawasim al-'Am min al-Waza'if.* Beirut: Dar Ibn Kathir, 1999.

: *Dhayl Tabaqat al-Hanabila.* Beirut: Dar al-Kutub al-'Ilmiyya, 1997.

- Khatib al-Baghdadi al-: *Tarikh Baghdad.* Beirut: Dar al-Gharb al-Islami, 2001.
- Sibt Ibn al-Jawzi: *Mir'at al-Zaman fi Tawarikh al-A'yan.* Damascus: Dar al-Risala, 2013.

- Sullami, Abu Abd al-Rahman Muhammad ibn al-Husayn al-: *Tabaqat al-Sufiyya*. Beirut: Dar al-Kutub al-'ilmiyya, 2003.

NOTES

1   Narrated by al-Hakim.

2   Narrated by Muslim in *Kitab al-Iman* from the report of Abu Hurayra, may Allah be well pleased with him.

3   Narrated by Tirmidhi.

4   Cf. Ibn Rajab al-Hanbali, *Lata'if al-Ma'arif*, p. 171.

5   Of these, one can mention *Ma'adin al-Ibriz fi Tafsir al-Kitab al-Aziz* and *al-Madhhab al-Ahmad fi Madhhab Ahmad*.

6   Imam al-Dhahabi mentioned in his *Siyar A'lam al-Nubala*, vol. 21: p. 375, that one of Ibn al-Jawzi's books is entitled: *al-Hath 'ala Talab al-Walad* [Prompting Others to Have Children].

7   Making supplications upon completing the recitation

of the whole Quran was a practice of the righteous Predecessors, may Allah be well pleased with them. It is reported, for instance, that, upon completing the recitation of the whole Quran, the Prophetic Companion Anas, may Allah be well pleased with him, used to gather his children and the members of his household and pray for them. This is narrated by al-Darimi and also by Abu Dawud through two rigorously authenticated chains of transmission as mentioned by Imam al-Nawawi in his book *al-Adhkar*.

8   The words of this sentence are a rigorously authentic Prophetic saying from the report of Ali ibn Abi Talib, may Allah be well pleased with him, which is narrated by al-Bukhari and Muslim.

9   Imam al-Dhahabi mentioned in *Tadhkirat al-Huffaz* that he knew of no scholar who has authored more books than Ibn al-Jawzi.

10   In *Siyar A'lam al-Nubala'*, these verses are attributed to al-Murtada, the father of Abul-Fada'il Muhammad ibn Abd Allah ibn al-Qasim ibn Muzaffar al-Shafi,

with substituting (by Allah) at the beginning of the first verse with (O night [Ya layl]).

11   Al-Baqara 2: 282.

12   Ibn al-Jawzi spoke about his high resolve in different places in his book *Sayd al-Khatir*.

13   Cf. Ibn Kathir, *al-Bidaya wa'l-Nihaya*, vol. 13: p. 29.

14   Abul-Fadl Muhammad ibn Nasir ibn Muhammad ibn Ali ibn Am al-Salammi al-Baghdadi (467-552 AH) was a Hadith master and Hafiz. He was Ibn al-Jawzi's teacher of Hadith. Cf. *Siyar A'lam al-Nubala*, vol. 20, p. 265, *Tadhkirat al-Huffaz*, vol. 4, p. 1289, *Manaqib Ahmad*, pp. 530-531, *Mir'at al-Zaman*, vol. 8, p. 138 and *Tabaqat al-Hanabila*, vol. 1, pp. 225-229.

15   For the different kinds of authorisation in Hadith, see: Muhammad Mustafa A'zami, *Studies in Hadith Methodology and Literature*. Kuala Lumpur: Islamic Book Trust, 2002, Ch. 3.

16   Ibn al-Jawzi writes in *Sayd al-Khatir*, p. 235: 'In the sweet savour of my quest for sacred knowledge, I faced hardships that were sweeter to me than honey, in view

of what I was seeking and hoping for. When I was a young lad, I used to take with me hard loaves of bread upon going out in pursuit of Hadith. [When it was time to eat,] I used to sit at the bank of the River 'Isa unable to swallow the bread unless I drank water with it, all while the eye of my resolve was focused on the pleasure of acquiring sacred knowledge. As a result, I became known for my abundant attendance of the sessions of transmission of the hadiths of the Messenger of Allah, may Allah bless him and grant him peace, his states, manners as well as of the states of his Companions and the generation that came after them. This also resulted in me adopting ways of dealing with Allah which can only be known through sacred knowledge. So much so that I remember, at times of strong sensual desire, when I was in my teenage years and away from home, the ease with which I could have engaged in things for which my ego was craving, like the craving of a thirsty person for cold water, but the fear of Allah which I acquired from learning sacred knowledge prevented me from doing so.'

17 The dhimmis are non-Muslims, usually Jews and Christians, permanently living in the lands of Islam. On some of the questions raised around this issue, see: Anver M. Emon, *Religious Pluralism and Islamic Law: Dhimmis and Others in the Empire of Law*. Oxford University Press, 2012.

18 Abu Ishaq al-'Ujali al-Khurasani al-Balkhi, better known as Ibrahim ibn Adham (c 100-c 165 AH/718-782 CE) was one of the greatest early Sufis. He was born in Balkh, present day Afghanistan, and lived and died in the Levant. Cf. *Hilyat al-Awliya'*, vol. 7, p. 367, *Tabaqat al-Awliya'*, vol. 5, p. 15 and *Siyar A'lam al-Nubala*, vol. 7, p. 387.

19 Imam Abu Amr al-Tamimi al-Anbari was a great saint and ascetic. He died during the reign of the first Umayyad caliph Muawiya ibn Abi Sufyan. Cf. *Hilyat al-Awliya*, vol. 2, p. 87 and *Siyar A'lam al-Nubala*, vol. 4, p. 15.

20 Abu Mahfuz al-Baghdadi Maruf al-Karkhi (d. 200

AH) was a great Sufi shaykh. Imam Ibn al-Jawzi wrote a whole book about his virtues while Imam Ahmad described him as someone whose supplications were always answered. Cf. *Tabaqat al-Awliya*, p. 280, *Tabaqat al-Sufiyya*, pp. 83-90, *Tabaqat al-Hanabila*, vol. I, p. 381 and *Hilyat al-Awliya*, vol. 8, p. 360.

21 Narrated by Ibn Abi Shayba in his *Musannaf* as well as Tirmidhi, Nasa'i, Ibn Hibban, al-Hakim and Abu Ya'la from the hadith of Jabir, may Allah be well pleased with him.

22 Abul-Hasan Kahmas ibn al-Hasan al-Tamimi was one of the greatest transmitters of Hadith and a righteous servant of Allah. He died in 149 AH. Cf. *Tadhkirat al-Huffaz*, vol. I, p. 174, *Siyar A'lam al-Nubala*, vol. 6, p. 316 and *Shadharat al-Dhahab*, vol. 1, p. 225.

23 Ibn al-Jawzi wrote in his *al-Yawaqit al-Jawziyya*, pp. 28-29: 'May Allah reward those people who forsook sweet sleep, fell to the ground out of exhaustion from the very matter they set themselves to achieve and stood upright in the darkness of night, seeking a share

of Divine Munificence. When the night falls, they stay awake; and when the day comes, they ponder and reflect; when they consider their faults, they seek refuge in Allah; and when they think about their sins, they weep and feel heartbroken. O dwellings of the beloved ones! Where are your inhabitants? O sites of sincerity! Where are your dwellers? O places of the godly! Where are your occupiers? O residences of pre-dawn prayers and supplication! Where are your visitors? By Allah, the land is deserted, the [sincere and godly] folk have disappeared, and those who stay awake at night have departed, leaving behind only those who prefer sleep, and fasting has been substituted with engaging in all kinds of desires.'

24 Umm al-Khayr bint Isma'il Rabi'a al-Adawiyya of Basra was a devout righteous woman who died in 180 AH at about the age of eighty. Cf. *Siyar A'lam al-Nubala*, vol. 8, p. 242, *Wafayat al-A'yan*, vol.3, p. 215, *Tarikh Baghdad*, vol. 2, p. 40 and *Sifat al-Safwa*, vol. 4, pp. 17-19. Ibn al-Jawzi wrote a whole book about the virtues

of this righteous woman.

25   Abu Hurayra, may Allah be well pleased with him, reported that the Messenger of Allah, may Allah bless him and grant him peace, said: 'The ages of my nation vary between sixty and seventy [years], only a minority amongst them exceeds this.' This hadith is narrated by Tirmidhi, Ibn Maja, Ibn Hibban and al-Hakim in his *Mustadrak*. The Prophet, may Allah bless him and grant him peace, also said: 'Allah leaves no excuse for a person whom Allah extends his age until he reaches sixty.' Narrated by al-Bukhari from the report of Abu Hurayra, may Allah be well pleased with him.

26   Abu Hakim Ibrahim ibn Dinar al-Nahrawani al-Hanbali was one of the imams of Baghdad who combined great erudition with God-consciousness. He earned his living working as a tailor. He was also known for serving the handicapped and the elderly with a cheerful mien. He died in 556 AH. Cf. *Siyar A'lam al-Nubala*, vol. 20, p. 396, *Dhayl Tabaqat al-Hanabila*, vol. 1, pp. 231-241 and *al-Bidaya wa'l-Nihaya*, vol. 12, p. 245.

27 Abu Abd Allah Muhammad ibn Ali ibn Muhammad ibn Hasan ibn Abd al-Wahhab ibn Hasawayh was born in Damghan, situated between Rayy and Nishapur, and was a great scholar, Mufti of Iraq and Chief Judge. He was compared in his days to Qadi Abu Yusuf. Many of his children were also scholars and judges. He died in 478 AH. Cf. *Tarikh Baghdad*, vol. 3, p. 109, *al-Bidaya wa'l-Nihaya*, vol. 12, p. 146, *Siyar A'lam al-Nubala*, vol. 18, p. 485.

28 The jurist Abd al-Rahman ibn Muhammad ibn Ali ibn Muhammad al-Halawani was one of the scholars of the Hanbali school of law who was also proficient in Quranic exegesis and Hadith. He authored a commentary on the Quran in forty-one volumes. Cf. *Dhayl Tabaqat al-Hanabila*, vol. 1, p. 221.

29 The shaykh of the Hanbalis Abu al-Khattab Mahfuz ibn Ahmad ibn Hasan ibn Hasan al-Iraqi who died in 510 AH was one of the greatest jurists and legal theorists, who combined knowledge and practice. He was known for his piety, excellent manners and wit. Cf.

Siyar A'lam al-Nubala, vol. 19, p. 348, *al-Muntazam*, vol. 9, pp. 190-193, *al-Bidaya wa'l-Nihaya*, vol. 12, p. 180, *Dhayl Tabaqat al-Hanabila*, vol. 1, pp. 116-127 and *Shadharat al-Dhahab*, vol. 4, pp. 27-28.

30   Narrated by al-Bukhari in *Kitab al-Da'awat* from the report of Hudhayfa, may Allah be well pleased with him, and from the report of Abu Dharr, may Allah be well pleased with him. It is also narrated by Muslim from the report of al-Bara' ibn 'Azib, may Allah be well pleased with him.

31   Narrated by Abu Ya'la in his *Musnad*, al-Nasa'i, Ibn al-Sunni, Ibn Hibban and al-Hakim, all from the report of Abul-Zubayr from Jabir.

32   The Mother of the Believers Aisha, may Allah be well pleased with her, said: 'The Prophet, may Allah bless him and grant him peace, was not committed to the upkeep of any supererogatory act as he was to the two units of *Fajr*.' Narrated by al-Bukhari and Muslim.

33   Narrated by Ahmad, Ibn Maja and Ibn al-Sunni.

34   Cf. *Sahih al-Bukhari, Kitab al-Adhan, Bab Maymanat*

al-Masjid wa'l-Imam.

35 Narrated by Ahmad from the report of Abu Ayyub al-Ansari, may Allah be well pleased with him.

36 Narrated by Abu Dawud, Tirmidhi and al-Nasa'i from the report of Abd Allah ibn Amr, may Allah be well pleased with him.

37 Narrated by Ibn al-Sunni from the report of Muhammad ibn Himyar from Muhammad ibn Ziyad from Abu Umama, who attributed it to the Prophet, may Allah bless him and grant him peace.

38 Umm Hani Fakhita bint Abi Talib, may Allah be well pleased with her, said: 'I went to visit the Messenger of Allah, may Allah bless him and grant him peace, on the year of the conquest of Mecca and found him performing major ritual ablution. When he finished his ablution, he prayed eight units of prayer. And the time was mid-morning.' Narrated by al-Bukhari and Muslim.

39 The Prophet, may Allah bless him and grant him peace, said: 'Keep preserving the Quran [in your hearts] for it slips away from the breasts of men more

easily than the cattle do from the cords used to hobble them.' Narrated by al-Bukhari and Muslim from the report of Abu Hurayra.

40 Cf. *Sahih al-Bukhari* (6315) and Muslim (2710).

41 This is in compliance with the hadith which is narrated by al-Bukhari and Muslim from the report of Ali ibn Abi Talib.

42 Narrated by Abu Dawud, Ibn al-Sunni, al-Nasa'i and al-Tabarani in *al-Mu'jam al-Kabir*.

43 This was stated by a number of eminent scholars including al-Zuhri, Sufyan al-Thawri, Abu Hanifa, al-Shafii and others. Ibn Rajab al-Hanbali wrote on this issue: 'This is a matter of contention between scholars: which one is better, seeking sacred knowledge or supererogatory prayer, recitation of the Quran and remembrance of Allah? As for the one who is sincere in his quest of sacred knowledge for the sake of Allah and is at the same time bright, seeking sacred knowledge is better for him on condition that he combines it with a share of prayer and other acts of worship. If

you see a person striving hard in his quest of sacred knowledge but has no share in acts of drawing closer to Allah, then you should know that this person is lazy and despicable and is not genuine in his intention. As for the person who seeks Hadith and jurisprudence for egotistic inclinations, then acts of worship are better for him… In sum, those who are sincere in their quest for sacred knowledge are few…'

44 For details about this point and the different arguments for and against it, see: The Proprieties of Seclusion in Abu Hamid al-Ghazali's *Revival of the Religious Sciences*.

45 Abu Muhammad Ata ibn Abi Rabah Aslam al-Qurashi, *Shaykh al-Islam* and Mufti of the Holy Mosque in Mecca, was born in Mecca during the reign of the Rightly-guided caliph Uthman ibn Affan, may Allah be well pleased with him. Despite his physical ailments – he was blind in one eye, flat-nosed and paralytic – he was one of the greatest scholars of Islamic law and Hadith in his generation. Cf. *Siyar*

A'lam al-Nubala, vol. 5, p. 78, *al-Bidaya wa'l-Nihaya*, vol. 9, p. 306, *Shadharat al-Dhahab*, vol.1, p. 147 and *al-'Iqd al-'Ihamin*, vol. 6, p. 84.

46　Sulayman ibn Abd al-Malik ibn Marwan ibn al-Hakam ibn Abi al-As ibn Umayya was sworn in as Caliph after his brother al-Walid in 99 AH. He remained in his office for less than three years. He was the one who appointed the fifth Rightly-Guided Caliph Umar ibn Abd al-Aziz as his heir and successor. Cf. *Tarikh al-Tabari*, vol. 6, p. 546, *al-Kamil* of Ibn al-Athir, vol. 5, p. 37, *al-Bidaya wa'l-Nihaya*, vol. 9, p. 183, *Shadharat al-Dhahab*, vol. 1, p. 116 and *Siyar A'lam al-Nubala*, vol. 5, p. 111.

47　Abu Sa'id al-Hasan ibn Abi Yasar, the client of Zayd ibn Thabit, was a Follower of the Prophetic Companions and a role model for all scholars and ascetics. It was said that his speech resembled the speech of prophets. He died in 110 AH. Cf. *Hilyat al-Awliya'*, vol. 2, p. 131, *Siyar A'lam al-Nubala*, vol. 4, p. 563, *al-Zuhd* of Imam Ahmad, vol. 2, p. 225, and *Tadhkirat al-Huffaz*, vol. 1, p. 66. Imam Ibn al-Jawzi wrote a separate book about his life and virtues.

48   Abu Bakr Muhammad ibn Sirin al-Ansari, was the client of the Prophetic Companion Anas ibn Malik, the servant of the Messenger of Allah, may Allah bless him and grant him peace. He died in 110 AH. Cf. *Hilyat al-Awliya*, vol. 2, p. 263, *Siyar A'lam al-Nubala*, vol. 4, p. 606, *Tadhkirat al-Huffaz*, vol. 1, p. 73 and *Tarikh Baghdad*, vol. 5, p. 331.

49   Makhul ibn Abi Aslam Shahrab ibn Shadhil ibn Sind ibn Shirwan ibn Yazdak ibn Yaghuth ibn Kisra (the Khosrow of Persia) was one of the greatest scholars of the Levant. He was a Follower of the Prophetic Companions. He died circa 112 AH. Cf. *Siyar A'lam al-Nubala*, vol. 5, p. 155, *Tadhkirat al-Huffaz*, vol. 1, p. 107 and *al-Bidaya wa'l-Nihaya*, vol. 9, p. 305.

50   In his commentary on the report of Abul-Darda, 'Whoever treads a path seeking knowledge therein...', Ibn Rajab al-Hanbali wrote: 'The person who diffuses his knowledge to people and addresses them ought to

be scrupulous about what they possess and not crave for anything of their wealth and possessions. Likewise he should not attempt to attract them towards himself. Rather, he should propagate his knowledge for the sake of Allah and abstain from what people have through scrupulousness... For being keen on this world and craving for it is despicable, and it is even more despicable coming from scholars of sacred knowledge'.

51 This story was mentioned by Ibn Rajab al-Hanbali in his commentary on the report of Abul-Darda, 'Whoever treads a path seeking knowledge therein...'

52 Narrated by Tirmidhi and Ahmad. Ibn Rajab al-Hanbali wrote a book on the explanation of this hadith entitled *Nur al-Iqtibas fi Mishkat Wasiyyat al-Nabi, Salla Allahu 'alayhi wa-Sallam li-ibn 'Abbas.*

53 Cf. *Hilyat al-Awliya.*

54 Narrated by al-Bukhari and Muslim from the report of Ibn Umar, may Allah be well pleased with father and son.

55 Abu Abd Allah Sufyan ibn Sa'id ibn Masruq al-Thawri

al-Kufi was an eminent scholar of Hadith and Islamic law as well as a great Sufi. He died in 261 AH. Cf. *Hilyat al-Awliya*, vol. 6, p.356, *Siyar A'lam al-Nubala*, vol. 7, p. 229 and *Tarikh Baghdad*, vol. 9, pp. 151-174.

56 Abu Muhammad Sa'id ibn al-Musayyib al-Qurashi al-Makhzumi the *Alim* of Madina and the chief companion of the Prophetic Companions of his time. He died in 73 AH. Cf. *Siyar A'lam al-Nubala*, vol. 4, p. 217, *Hilyat al-Awliya*, vol. 2, p. 161, and *Tadhkirat al-Huffaz*, vol. 1, p. 51.

57 One of the greatest scholars of Islam, and the founder of one of the four Islamic legal schools. He was renowned for his knowledge, piety and steadfastness in the face of coercion. He was imprisoned and tortured for defending the beliefs of Orthodox Islam against the heresies of the Mu'tazilites, who had royal backing.

58 This book is in print in several editions and by different publishing houses.

59 This was perhaps at the time of writing the present epistle; otherwise some scholars have enumerated

more than one thousand titles which can be checked in *Siyar A'lam al-Nubala* and *Dhayl Tabaqat al-Hanabila*. See also Abd al-Hamid al-Aluji, *Mu'allafat Ibn al-Jawzi*, Baghdad, 1975.

60 Ibn al-Jawzi later abridged this book into four volumes which he entitled *Zad al-Masir fi 'Ilm al-Tafsir*.

61 It is reported that Umar ibn Abd al-Aziz, may Allah be well pleased with him, said: 'Whoever acts without a basis of knowledge will cause more harm than benefit.' Narrated by Ibn Abd al-Barr in *Jami Bayan al-Ilm* and Ibn Abi Shayba in his *Musannaf*. Likewise, al-Hasan al-Basri, may Allah have mercy on him, said: 'Seek sacred knowledge in a way that does not harm your devotion to worship and devote yourself to worship in a manner that does not harm your quest for sacred knowledge. For he who acts without knowledge causes more harm than benefit.'

62 This title could be the same as *Minhaj al-Qasidin* by Ibn al-Jawzi himself, an abridgment of which is in print. All the other titles mentioned in this chapter

are Ibn al-Jawzi's.

63 In this book, Ibn al-Jawzi recorded all the ideas and thoughts that suddenly occurred to him so as not to forget them. The book is in three volumes and has been printed in several different editions.

64 Imam al-Dhahabi mentioned that this book is in two volumes.

65 The full title is: *al-Kashf li-Mushkil al-Sahihayn*, and it is in two volumes.

66 Ibn al-Jawzi wrote in his *al-Qussas wal-Mudhakkirin*: 'I have compiled books on the tools of preaching, the like of which I do not think anyone has written, exegeses of the Quran which are free of lapses and fabricated traditions, such as *Zad al-Masir fi Ilm al-Tafsir* and *al-Mughni,* which is more voluminous... As for the books on preaching, they are too many to enumerate, including *Tabsirat al-Mubtadi'*, *Kanz al-Mudhakkir*, *al-Lu'lu'*, *al-Mulah*, *al-Mudhish*, *al-Mulhib*, *Saba Najd*, *Nasim al-Riyad*, *al-Muntakhab* and others. Some of these

books are all that any preacher may need and are sufficient for him all his life.'

67 Ibn al-Jawzi wrote in *Sayd al-Khatir* (p. 232): 'I know of no pleasure, triumph, honour, rest or safety for the scholar of sacred knowledge better than seclusion. Through seclusion, he obtains the safety of his body, religion and status with Allah as well as with people. This is because people take liberties with the person who mixes with them and never appreciate his importance. This is why, due to their seclusion, kings and rulers are highly venerated by ordinary people. When common people see a scholar of sacred knowledge engaged in something legally indifferent (*mubah*), they take him lightly. Hence, it is necessary for the scholar to safeguard his knowledge and establish the importance of sacred knowledge in their eyes. One righteous predecessor said: "We used to joke and laugh about. But once we became role models for others, we no longer thought it behove us to do so."'

68 It is mentioned in a Prophetic saying: 'That you leave

your heirs rich is better than leaving them dependent on others, seeking their sufficiency from people.' Narrated by al-Bukhari and Muslim from the hadith of Sa'd ibn Abi Waqqas, may Allah be well pleased with him.

69 Ibn al-Jawzi's full lineage is as follows: Abul-Faraj Abd al-Rahman ibn Ali ibn Muhammad ibn Ali ibn Ubayd Allah ibn Abd Allah ibn Hammadi ibn Ahmad ibn Muhammad ibn Ja'far ibn Abd Allah ibn al-Qasim ibn al-Nadr ibn al-Qasim ibn Muhammad ibn Abd Allah ibn Abd al-Rahman the *faqih* ibn al-Qasim the *faqih* ibn Muhammad ibn Abu Bakr al-Siddiq the caliph of the Messenger of Allah, may Allah bless him and grant him peace.

70 He was one of the greatest scholars of his time, alongside Salim and Ikrima. He was born during the reign of Ali ibn Abi Talib, may Allah be well pleased with him, and raised by his paternal aunt the Mother of the Believers, Aisha, may Allah be well pleased with her, from whom he learnt *fiqh*. He died in 70 AH. Cf. *Hilyat al-Awliya*, vol. 2, p. 183; *Tadhkirat al-Huffaz*, vol.

1, p. 96, *Siyar A'lam al-Nubala*, vol. 5, p.54 , *Shadharat al-Dhahab*, vol. 1, p. 135 and *Sifat al-Safwa*, vol. 2, p. 88.